HOW TO
DRAW & PAINT
THE FIGURE

CONTENTS

Introduction	4
Oil	6
Acrylic	24
Watercolor	32
Tempera	40
Pastel	42
Pencil	46
Pen and Ink	56

Figure

THE IDEALIZATION OF man has long been a preoccupation of art as has the description of man's miseries: the Greek sculptors with their 'perfect form' or the agonies endured by Goya's subjects; Boucher's plump, seductive women, or the tense and anxious characters in a Giacometti. Nude or clothed, alone or in groups, the figure has always been a vehicle for expression, whether of tender compassion, or bitterness and anger. Every picture which includes the human form invariably carries within it a dimension beyond other types of art, a comment or reflection upon the character of the individual or on the condition of man. It need not be deliberate, indeed, it often is not, but it *is* inescapable. Man describing man always involves visual interpretation and this can be used to the artist's advantage.

The Egyptians used the human form as symbols in the religious and social organization of their society. For centuries there was virtually no change in these figurative symbols which were instantly recognizable and unmistakable. The concept of foreshortening, which assumes a knowledge of perspective, escaped these early artists. Thus limbs were de-scribed as if seen in profile so that legs and feet appear in side view, attached to a frontal view of the torso. Heads turn to show a profile because this is the most characteristic shape.

The differences between Egyptian and Greek art were the result of fundamental philosophical and political divisions. The great advance in the depiction of the human form came with the Renaissance, and particularly with the close study of human anatomy. Figures were to become used in a thousand ways for as many different reasons; religious themes remained for centuries but, in due time, more secular needs were also met. The 17th century painter Rubens was a master at rendering the fleshy nudes fashionable in his day and indeed he ran a workshop/studio which produced large scenes of classical and other subjects, with many a nude cavorting. The 19th century painter Fragonard dealt with the themes dear to the heart of the French courtiers – the shimmering world of high life at court. William Etty (1787–1849) was an English artist who painted virtually nothing but the figure, the fleshy surfaces of his nudes cunningly rendered. Into the 19th century the paintings of Courbet, magnificent in their compos-

Proportions The figures show a comparison of the male and female form, front and back. Comparative anatomy is an important aspect of all figure work, and by contrasting the male and female forms, a better understanding of each can be gained. Note the downward slope of the female shoulder, lower waistline and broader hips. The rear view shows the female to have a lower center of gravity than the male. All of these aspects influence the human body regardless of its size or position.

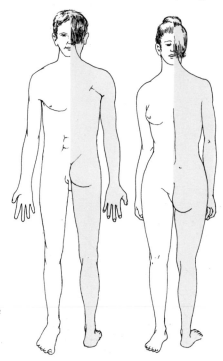

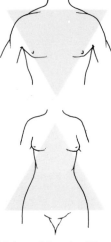

Male and female The human figure represented by a triangle. In the male, broad shoulders narrow to the hips. In the female, shoulders broaden to the hips.

ition and structure, contain supreme examples of figure painting, as do those of Millet.

Painting and drawing the figure

The practical problems of figure painting and drawing are in some ways similar to those of portraiture, but include other aspects as well. When studying works in galleries, always look to find the individual ways used to relate the figures, both to each other and to the background. Consider how the feeling you have for the subject can best be expressed through color – stark and harsh, or of a languid, linear quality. Note the way Ingres used colour to inspire life into his pictures or the seductive flow in a Modigliani nude; observe the nudes in paint and pastel by Degas, with their energy and liveliness.

Make sure that in selecting subjects and ideas for compositions, you are convinced about the content, for example, whether it is contemporary or classical in theme. Nothing shows more clearly than the uncommitted idea, forced out of the artist and on to the canvas. Diebenkorn, a contemporary American artist, is a good example of a figure painter with a convincing ring to the content of his works.

The palettes recommended for portrait painting will also be found suitable for painting nudes, and the techniques of generalized underpainting brought to a finer focus via scumbling and glazing, for example, will prove useful in both cases. Our demonstrations show how these methods can be used, and experimenting with them in personal ways will prove invaluable. When using pencil, try varying both pencil quality and paper surface. A hard lead on medium textured paper will allow for a good range of marks, but remember that the scale of the work will alter the overall view. Pen and ink techniques abound. See how a simple, precise line or a hatched tone of black lines best relate the story you wish to tell. Smudging or applying washes to pen and ink figure drawings can increase the subtleties and allow for greater definition. Mixed media pictures involving single figures or groups of figures should be ventured; pencil will do some things that pen or paint cannot, and as well, the reverse holds true. As always, the best way of learning is through experimentation. There are few rules, and these should be approached only as guidelines.

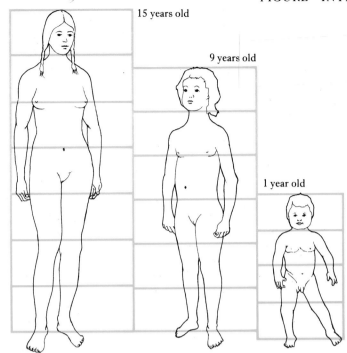

15 years old

9 years old

1 year old

Age and size The human is measured in heads. As the body grows in height, the proportions change accordingly. Left: The child of 1 year is 4 heads high. Center: The 9 year old is 6 heads. Far left: the 15 year old is 7 heads high.

Auguste Renoir, 'Woman's Torso in Sunlight'. Renoir is renowned for his sensuous nudes.

5

Oil

ONE OF the beauties of working in acrylics is that the artist can use them as a short-cut for the under-painting of oils with-out losing any of the brilliance of tra-ditional oil underpainting. The artist can work quickly to block in general shapes and tones as a rough version to work from, or he can develop the underpainting to a nearly complete state and then finish off in oils. While at first glance this painting may seem to involve sophisticated color mixes and brushwork, most of the subtlety of tone and coloring is derived from the underpainting and the layering of thin washes of color one upon the other.

It is important to remember that the underpainting, whether executed in oil or acrylic, will have a strong effect on the finished picture. This is logical when you consider that the majority of drawings and paintings are done on white canvas to allow the pure, true brilliance of the color – regardless of media – to come through. No matter how thick, or opaque the paint mix-ture, the underpainting will affect the tones with subtle hints of color. The glass behind the figure is a good example of this, as nearly all the layers of color are in some way apparent in the finished picture.

Materials

Surface
Stretched and primed canvas

Size
27 in × 30 in (67 cm × 75 cm)

Tools
Nos 4, 6, and 10 flat bristle brushes
No 4 round sable brush
Palette

Colors

Acrylic:	Oils:
Cadmium red	Alizarin crimson
Cadmium yellow	Black
Hansa yellow	Cadmium red light
Mars black	Cadmium yellow
Pthalo green	Raw umber
Titanium white	Ultramarine blue
Ultramarine blue	White

Mediums
Water
Turpentine
Copal oil

1. With acrylic colors cadmium red, pthalo green and hansa yellow, apply the underpainting in a wet wash with a No 10 brush. Lay in general shadows.

2. Mix ultramarine blue and alizarin crimson and with a sable brush and ruler, put in the grid on the door.

6. Mix white and blue and with a No 6 brush work into the background area. With white and burnt umber, put in the woodwork and window.

7. With a No 4 brush mix oil colours cadmium red, yellow and a little blue for flesh tones. Mix black and blue and block in the hair. Use red for flowers.

Drawing the grid · blocking in hair · details

3. Mix hansa yellow and cadmium red in a wet wash and with the No 10 brush, cover door and flesh areas. Outline the figure with a small brush and burnt umber.

4. Put in the dark areas of the dress in a mixture of black and ultramarine blue. With an opaque orange, put in the reflections in the door and blend.

5. Mix a thin wash of orange and water and glaze over the face. With opaque white and a No 4 sable brush, block in the highlights in the face and blend lightly.

8. With a No 4 sable brush and pale blue, put in the hair highlights. Define the profile with burnt umber. Add touches of blue around the eyes for shadow areas.

9. Mix yellow ochre and white and put in warm highlight tones of the face. Blend a very light tone into the jawline. Add red and carry down the neck and chest.

10. Mix a pale tone from blue, white and umber and rub into the background. Heighten the reflection colors in the glass and blend. *(continued overleaf)*

After the underpainting has dried thoroughly, the grid on the door is drawn in using a ruler, fine pointed sable brush, and dark paint. Allowing the brush to drag across the rough canvas varies the tone of the line.

Working back into the cool underpainting of the face, the artist is here blocking in the hair and shadow areas with a thin wash of blue-black acrylic paint.

With a small brush and dark paint, the artist works over the dried underpainting indicating folds in the fabric and dress patterns.

Redefining grid · highlighting · refining profile

Redefining grid · highlighting · refining profile

With a small sable brush and a light tone of grey, the artist puts in hair highlights using light quick strokes.

The original lines of the grid are redefined mid-way through the painting process.

Again using the small sable brush and opaque black paint, the profile of the sitter is cleaned up and further strengthened.

11. With the No 4 sable brush and a blue-black paint mixture, redefine the grid in the door with the ruler. Mix orange and water and glaze over the face.

13. With the same flesh tone, add a touch of green and lightly describe reflections in the mirror. Mix white, black, and blue and work over the light area behind the figure.

15. Put in the reflection of the hat with cadmium red. With white and yellow ochre, put in arm highlights

12. Mix a light tone of white and cadmium red and work back into the face, strengthening highlights with a small brush.

14. With orange and white, block in the arm. Work back into the reflections heightening light areas. Then, with black and blue, strengthen reflections

16. With a sable brush, put in details of hair and feather in hat. Strengthen highlight reflections in mirror with white and orange mixture.

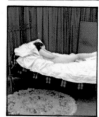

IN THIS painting the artist has let his imagination determine the techniques used. Rather than simply copying what was in front of him, elements of the subject have been used to create an interesting and atmospheric picture. While the artist used the subject largely for the preliminary stages of the painting, there was constant reference made to the model in the course of the work. Although the colors chosen are different from the actual subject, the artist used the general tones, highlights, and shadow areas within the model as reference and inspiration.

The painting was begun using the traditional technique of spreading a thin wash of color and turpentine over the surface to determine general tones and overall composition. It is interesting to note that the artist used brushes only for small areas of detail; the main body of the painting was executed with various shaped and sized palette knives. These allow a thick, opaque, juicy mixture of paint to be laid down and are especially useful for covering large areas. While it is difficult to render fine details with palette knives, the texture they create plus the broad planes of color can add a new dimension to an otherwise traditional technique.

Materials

Surface
Linen canvas, stretched and primed

Size
24in × 30in (60cm × 75cm)

Tools
Nos 4 and 8 flat bristle brushes
Assorted palette knives
Palette

Colors
Black   Gold ochre
Cadmium red medium   Lead white
Cerulean blue   Terre verte
Cobalt blue   Yellow ochre

Mediums
Turpentine
Linseed oil

1. With a No 8 brush, block in color areas with cerulean blue and light grey in a thin wash. Draw in the subject in pencil and blend colors with a small rag.

2. Use willow charcoal to reinforce outlines. Add more cerulean blue to color areas and blend. Put down charcoal and blend with turpentine and rag.

3. Mix cerulean blue and white and with a small palette knife lay in the figure and bed. Mix white, cerulean blue and black and describe the background and floor.

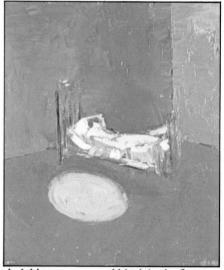

4. Add terre verte and block in the floor with a palette knife covering the surface. Work back into the walls, covering them thoroughly with the knife.

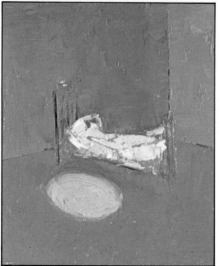

5. With pure white, brush in the figure and bed with a No 4 brush, covering the previous blue layer.

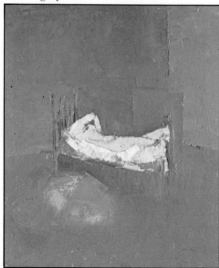

6. With a small palette knife, blend the rug out of the floor area. Lay in shadow areas with a darker floor tone and brush.

Finished picture · blocking in color · using palette knife · background area

The finished picture shows an interesting and innovative use of composition and technique. In particular this painting illustrates how a non-traditional approach to figure painting can yield interesting results.

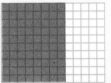

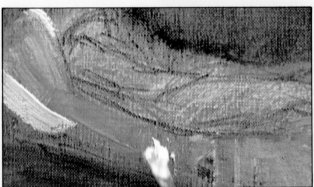

After the initial sketch has been described in charcoal, the artist begins to block in broad areas of color. The paint is allowed to bleed into the charcoal drawing. If this is not desirable, first dust the drawing lightly with a rag.

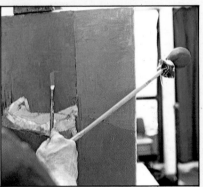

Using a Mahl stick and thin palette knife, the artist is here shown developing the background area.

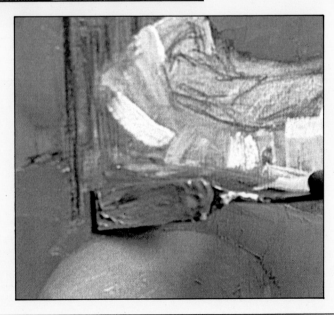

With a broad palette knife and a rich paint mixture, the artist puts in a layer of grey to describe the floor area.

FIGURE PAINTING is a highly individual process. There must be rapport between artist and sitter, or the painting will fail to capture the characteristics of both. It is important to remember that, while the artist is attempting to capture a superficial likeness, he is also trying to portray the essence, or personality, of the sitter as well. These aspects of portraiture should always determine the techniques used.

In this painting the artist has relied more on instinct than analysis and planning. This method requires self-confidence; it is not easy to boldly lay in free strokes without some anxiety over the outcome. With oil, however, if the artist lays down the wrong colour or shape, this can be easily scraped away and worked over.

The composition of this work is one of its outstanding features. The boldness of the colors and strokes and the oddly shaped chair arms serve to subtly emphasize the smallness of the figure without overpowering it and draw the eye inward.

By changing the background from white to taupe the artist has allowed the highlights and features of the child's face to come forward. The loose, white stroke at the bottom of the child's feet is repeated in the sleeves, and the odd shape emphasizes the natural liveliness of the subject.

Materials

Surface
Stretched and primed canvas

Size
18in × 20in (45cm × 50cm)

Tools
Nos 4 and 6 bristle brushes
No 2 sable brush
Palette

Colors

Burnt sienna	New blue
Cadmium green	Scarlet lake
Cadmium red deep	White
Chrome green	Yellow ochre

Mediums
Turpentine
Linseed oil

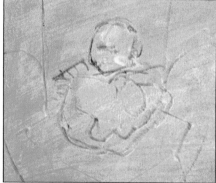

1. Mix burnt sienna and turpentine and with a small rag, rub into the surface. Dip a small No 2 sable brush in blue for outlines of figure and background.

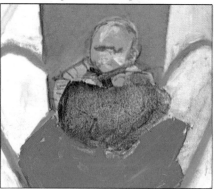

3. Using cadmium green, block in chair seat with a No 6 brush. Put in arms of chair in red with a No 4 brush. Block in white background and blend.

5. With the same colour used for the face, put in the shadow of the chair. Mix white with cadmium red and put in chair highlights and blend with brush or rag.

7. Work back into the clothes with the skin tone, indicating highlights. Add touches of red to the face and details in a greenish tone with a small brush.

2. With a No 4 bristle brush, block in the background with a thin wash of cadmium red. Thin blue and put in clothes. Use red and ochre for face.

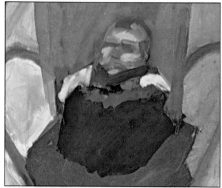

4. Block in blue clothes in ultramarine. Use same white as for background to describe the arms. Rework the face with a mixture of ochre, white, and cadmium red.

6. With a very loose stroke, put in white pattern at bottom of figure. With another brush, put in sleeve details with ultramarine blue and define features.

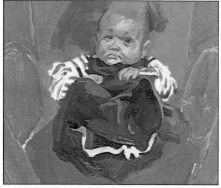

8. Mix burnt sienna, white, and red and cover the background. Use the same color in the face to strengthen shadow areas.

Finished picture· chair arms · facial details · blending with fingers

Besides employing a unique painting technique, the finished painting shows how much an interesting composition can add to any image. Especially in pictures of this type where the goal is to draw the viewer's eyes into the subject, attention should be paid to the placement of the figure.

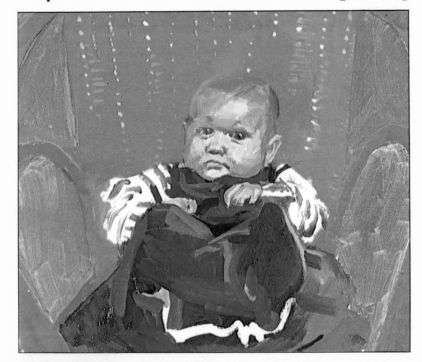

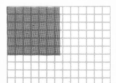

Fingers are often useful tools for creating an interesting texture and stroke. After applying paint directly from the tube the artist here smooths out the color with a finger.

With a fine sable brush, the artist works back into the face to describe details. If the paint surface is still wet, these small lines of color can then be blended with a clean, dry brush.

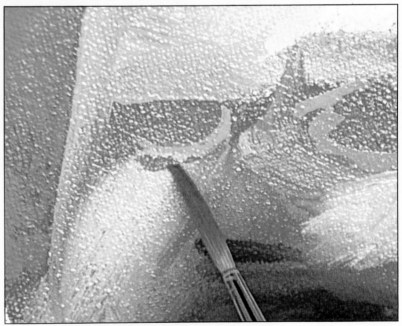

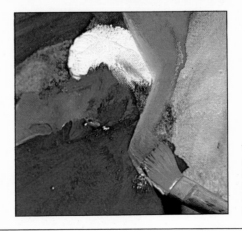

Working over the dry underpainting, the artist blocks in the arms of the chair beside the child's right elbow.

13

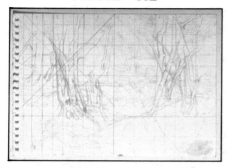

THE TECHNIQUE USED in this painting is a unique one which combines a number of extremely old painting methods. Fresco, tempera, and miniature painting techniques are all used, the results showing the inherent beauty of all of them. The basic technique is known as 'wet white'.

Because the artist must work in concentrated areas of detail – much like doing a needlepoint – this technique requires patience and a steady hand. It is a slow process and only very small areas can be covered at a time – thus its similarity to Renaissance fresco painting where only one area of a wall was worked on in the course of a day. The artist first mixes flake white and copal varnish, and applies a small amount to the surface. With a very fine sable brush and a touch of oil color thinned with turpentine, he then stipples a small area of color on to the white. The white/varnish mixture has the effect of bringing forth a jewel-like quality in the paint, which lends translucence and depth to the overall effect.

Until the paint dries, the area worked on is flexible and movable. It can be altered, corrected or worked on until the paint dries – approximately a day. If the artist is dissatisfied with the results, he can overpaint, but this must be done while the paint is wet.

Materials

Surface
Primed hardboard

Size
12in (30cm) diameter

Tools
Nos 2 and 4 sable brushes
Palette or plate

Colors
Alizarin crimson	Cerulean blue
Cadmium green	Cobalt blue
Cadmium red	Flake white
Cadmium yellow	

Mediums
Copal oil varnish
Turpentine

Finished picture
overpainting with white · pure color strokes · brushstrokes

The special technique used to create this picture is best understood through the use of close-up shots of the work. For this reason, the picture has not been presented in steps.

A thin layer of flake white and copal varnish are laid down over the transferred drawing. While still wet, using a fine sable brush and ultramarine blue, the artist stipples in dots of paint, following the pencil outline.

Rather than mixing colors separately on a palette, this technique involves creating colors and tones directly on the surface by overlaying thin strokes of pure color.

This detail shows the particular brushstrokes required when using the 'wet white' technique. Note in particular the small touches of complementary color applied with small, light touches over the green underpainting to create depth.

PRECISION AND METHOD are the key-words for the technique used in this painting. Each area is painted in some detail so that the whole image gradually emerges piece by piece. At each new stage, the previous work is adjusted to ensure that the color and tonal relationships of the whole image are balanced

The range of color is limited and the palette consists primarily of earth colors. Cool grey shadows contrast with warm tones within the figure and these warm tones are enlivened by touches of vermilion. The dark greys in the chair and background wall are mixed from black and white, with the addition of ultramarine.

Use masking tape to establish clean outlines. Lay broad strips along the straight lines and define curves with narrow tape which can be manipulated into irregular shapes. Rub down the edges of the tape firmly before you paint over it and lay in areas of flat colour with large bristle brushes. Pull off the tape slowly and carefully to leave a clean, sharp edge.

Materials

Surface
Stretched and primed cotton duck

Size
39in × 30in (98 cm × 76cm)

Tools
HB Pencil
No 8 round sable brush
Nos 3, 7 flat bristle brush
Palette
1in (2.5cm), ¼in (.62cm) masking tape

Colors

Black	Vermilion
Burnt sienna	White
Burnt umber	Yellow ochre
Raw umber	

Medium
Turpentine

1. Lightly outline the composition with an HB pencil. With a No 8 sable brush, work into the face and hair with black and mixtures of sienna, vermilion, and white.

2. With a No 7 brush, block in flesh tones over the forehead and black and burnt umber in the hair. Work on details around eyes and nose with light browns.

6. Paint in the dark shadows on the chair with a mixture of burnt umber and black. Mask off the lines of the floor and chair legs with tape and block in dark brown.

7. Develop the background using masking tape to make straight lines. Fill in the shapes with yellow ochre and a dark red-brown directly behind the figure.

Masking tape · background · face and chair details

Masking tape can be useful for creating sharp, clean edges (below). When working with irregular shapes, use a narrow tape which can be manipulated into curves.

With a small brush, the artist blocks in the background area around the figure.

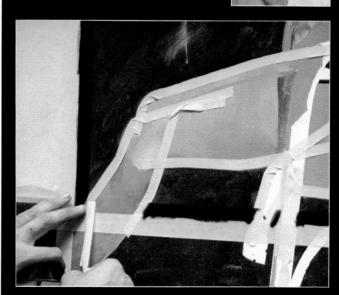

3. Build up the shape of the face with light pink tones and brown shadows, blending the colors together. Emphasize the mouth and nose with vermilion and white.

4. Work over the body putting in lines of shadow with burnt umber and blending flesh tones into the shapes. Draw up the hands and block in solid color.

5. Use a No 7 bristle brush to lay in broad areas of tone in the legs. Adjust colors over the entire figure and add strong white highlights.

8. Work over the rest of the background with a warm, pale beige, thinly shadowed with grey. Paint a thick layer of light grey over the chair and wall to right.

9. Work back over the head of the figure with a No 3 brush. Lay in a thin grey shape behind the model to depict shadow.

10. Brush in folds and creases on the jacket in black and blend with thick white paint to make mid-toned greys. Build up the woven pattern of the chair in white.

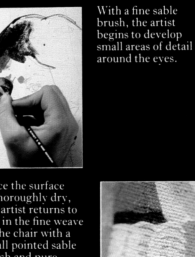

With a fine sable brush, the artist begins to develop small areas of detail around the eyes.

Once the surface is thoroughly dry, the artist returns to put in the fine weave of the chair with a small pointed sable brush and pure white paint.

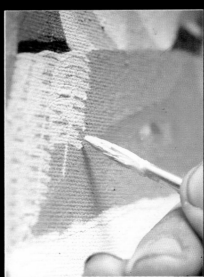

WHILE MOST of the activity in this painting centers around the figure and the chair as the central objects, the surrounding area also plays a crucial part in the success of the work as a whole.

By following through the steps, the method used by the artist becomes clear. Whether working on shadow areas or highlights, figure or background, blending and softening or defining and accentuating, the painting evolves through the constant and deliberate interplay of colors between figure and background. In looking carefully at the finished painting, you will see that all the colors used in the background are also contained in the figure. The broad planes of color describing floor and walls all move toward the figure, where they are concentrated, emphasized and modulated. The artist worked over the entire surface simultaneously; the figure was never altered without changing the environment, and vice versa.

The geometric shapes of the background – the strong verticals, horizontals and diagonals – emphasize the softness of the figure as a soft, malleable feature in a world of planes and edges. The warm tones in the figure and chair serve to separate it from its environment, which is predominantly cool and impersonal.

Materials

<u>Surface</u>
Prepared canvas board

<u>Size</u>
18in × 24in (45cm × 60cm)

<u>Tools</u>
No 10 round sable brush
No 4 flat bristle brush
Palette

<u>Colors</u>

Alizarin crimson	Chrome oxide
Burnt sienna	Raw sienna
Burnt umber	Ultramarine blue
Cadmium red	Yellow ochre

<u>Mediums</u>
Linseed oil
Turpentine

1. Mix burnt sienna and white. With a No 10 sable brush, block in the figure. With burnt umber, block in the ground area.

2. Add white to the burnt umber and start to block in the area surrounding the figure. Using the same mixture, begin to develop shadow areas within the figure.

4. Dip a No 4 brush in linseed oil and blend the previous color areas within the figure. Cover the remaining background area in green mixture.

5. Apply cadmium red directly from tube on to chair. Mix green and ochre and blend with rag or finger. Use a lighter tone of same in the background.

7. Mix alizarin crimson, blue and white and rework shadow areas in figure and background. Carry this into the foreground with a flicking motion.

8. Mix chrome green, white, and a touch of red and block in shape on the right. Carry this into the background. Lighten with white and use for highlights.

3. Mix chrome green and white and put in background. Apply cadmium red medium for the chair: white and ochre for highlights, and burnt umber for hair.

6. Mix red and white and put in the chair highlights. Carry this into the figure for highlight areas. Use pure burnt sienna to describe shape at left.

9. Develop final details of painting with white and yellow ochre. Mix white and umber for face features. With chrome green and yellow put in strip on left.

Blotting with tissue

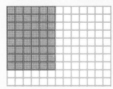

If the paint surface becomes too wet, excess moisture can be blotted up with a small piece of tissue. Do not rub into the surface but simply press the tissue down lightly.

IN ORDER to bring out the full tonal qualities of the subject, here the artist has used a narrow range of colors, relying on strong light and dark contrasts to disrupt what would otherwise be a predictable harmony. The result is a powerful image in which the figure is clearly recognizable, but with an element of abstraction in the pattern of the shadow and the broad planes of color.

The pattern of shapes in a painting is a crucial factor, so you should map out the composition carefully at the start. Follow the outlines as you apply the paint but keep the brushwork loose and vigorous. Thin the paint with turpentine and use long-handled bristle brushes in fluid strokes, gradually tightening up the image as the painting develops.

Color must be used carefully to differentiate the dark tones as otherwise the shapes will merge together. Enrich the heavy shadows by adding blue or brown to black paint. Adjust light tones continuously until you are satisfied with the result. Note that here the light yellow has been made more vivid in the final stage and extended over the orange shape to cool the contrast. None of the highlights are made from pure white and the intensity of the image is maintained through the relationship of the colors and the tones rather than through light and dark areas.

Materials

Surface
Stretched and primed cotton duck

Size
36in × 30in (90cm × 76cm)

Tools
No 6 flat bristle brushes
No 6 round sable brush
1in (2.5cm) decorators' brush
Palette

Colors
Black	Raw umber
Burnt sienna	Ultramarine blue
Burnt umber	Vermilion
Cadmium yellow	Yellow ochre

Medium
Turpentine

1. Sketch in the outlines with an HB pencil and then draw with a No 6 sable and black paint, using line and small areas of tone to establish the basic structure.

2. Draw up the central shadow across the figure with burnt sienna. Work into the flesh tones on the face and lay in the dark shadow behind the head.

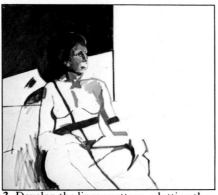

3. Develop the linear pattern, plotting the contour of the figure and shadows. Work into the face in more detail and block in a solid background tone.

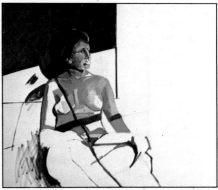

4. Using mixtures of burnt sienna and white with red and yellow, develop tones within the figure.

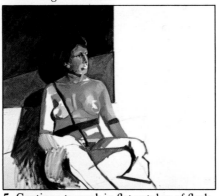

5. Continue to work in flat patches of flesh tones, brushing the colors together. Lay in reddish-brown behind the figure and dark blue shadows with a No 6 bristle.

6. Mix yellow ochre with raw umber and use a No 6 brush to block in the right-hand side of the background. Cover the white space, scrubbing into the canvas.

7. Work over the lower half of the figure with loose brushstrokes in dark brown tones. Contrast the shadows with a light yellow tone showing the fall of light.

8. Enrich the foreground colour with a solid shape of bright orange and warm tones in the legs, covering the remaining canvas. *(continued overleaf)*

Shadow areas · eye highlights · flesh tones

The shadow area beside the head is created with a dark tone thinned with turpentine. This is later covered over with a thicker layer of paint. The painting should develop through many thin layers of overpainting rather than a few thick layers.

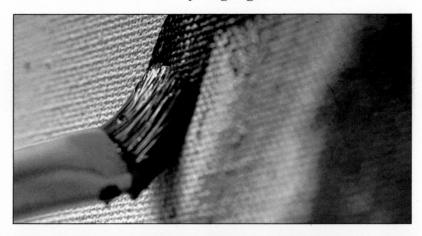

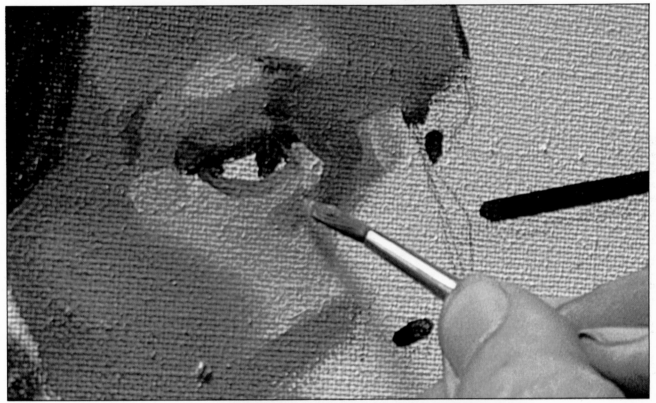

With a fine sable brush, the artist puts in highlight areas around the eye.

A mid-toned flesh color is blended into a shadow and highlight area. The paint is first laid down and then blended by using a clean, dry brush.

Figure shadows and blending

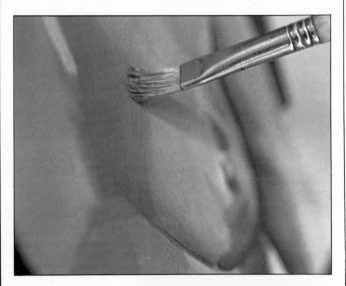

Shadow areas in the torso are described with a medium-sized sable brush. This color area is next blended into surrounding colors.

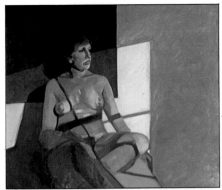

9. Revise the skin tones in the upper part of the figure, smoothly blending the color.

10. Continue to work over the whole image making adjustments in the color values. Lay in a dark blue-black shadow down the right leg of the figure.

11. Lighten the tones across the central section of the painting and even out patches of loosely worked color, blending them into smooth, fluid shapes.

12. Break down the foreground shapes to show the pattern of cast shadow over the legs. Strengthen dark tones with black and dark blue.

Acrylic

THE ARRANGEMENT OF a posed figure is important in that it is a means of providing the artist with a range of information from which a personal view can be formed. The artist should consider how to place the model, what kind of furniture and props to use, the direction and fall of the light, and the overall pattern of shapes and colors. In this case a mirror has been placed behind the model to give a back view of the pose and lighten the background tones.

Once the painting is started there is no need to adhere rigidly to every detail; let the work develop freely so your own particular interest in the subject can emerge.

The texture and strong color of acrylic paints provides good covering power and each layer can be built up rapidly without colors bleeding through from underneath. As the paint dries it forms a tough, erasery skin which cannot be scraped back or wiped off, so alterations must be made by overpainting with solid, opaque color.

Materials

Surface
Prepared canvas board

Size
24in × 20in (60cm × 50cm)

Tools
No 5 flat bristle brush
No 6 round sable brush
Palette

Colors

Alizarin crimson	Monastral blue
Black	Vermilion
Cadmium yellow medium	Violet
Chrome green	White

Medium
Water

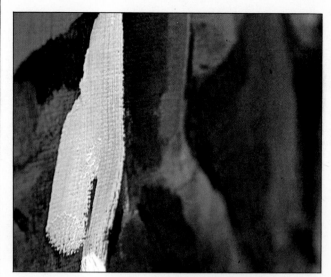

Preliminary colors · reinforcing outlines

Once the underpainting has dried thoroughly, the artist blocks in predominant color areas with a thick, opaque paint mixture.

After the tones of the figure have been laid in with a thin wash, the outlines are reinforced with a small brush and black paint.

1. Using red, yellow and blue, draw up the basic outline of the composition with a No 5 brush. Apply broad areas of tone and colour with thin, wet paint.

2. Add more detail to the structure of the drawing and break down tones into a more complex pattern.

6. Lay in a thin wash of red paint over the figure to warm up the colors. Draw up the face in detail and apply highlights with pinks and yellows.

7. Rework the figure with a No 8 sable brush, heightening the color and developing the forms. Paint details of the bed and drapery, blocking in darkest tones.

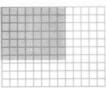

3. Work over the composition with line and thin washes of paint.

4. Apply the paint more thickly, using pinks and browns to build up the shape of the figure. Lay in a dark tone behind the head and shoulder.

5. Darken the background tone over the whole painting and contrast this with strong areas of white highlight.

8. Contrast light and dark tones in the figure showing the play of light over the form. Use light pinks and yellows to highlight against dark red and purple.

9. Work up the detail in the background showing the form and texture of the objects.

10. Use the final stages of the painting to make any alterations that come to mind. Use thick paint to lay in fresh detail or paint out shapes.

FIGURE painting is one of the major aspects of basic training in art schools. This is largely because it is a very flexible vehicle for the study of form and color. Many artists will work from one particular model over a period of time, as the range of paintings and drawings depicting different poses and elements can be almost infinite.

The primary factor in this composition is the luminous quality of the colors and tones. The model posed in a glass-walled studio on a bright, sunny day. The direct light gave a warm glow to the flesh tones of the figure. This warmth is represented at first in the painting with intense pinks and reds, but the full glowing effect becomes apparent as the colors are lightened and given a strong yellow cast. The shadows on the figure are painted mainly with dark green. This produces a more vibrant effect against the warm colors and forms a pictorial link with the heavy mass of green in the background foliage.

The essential factor is the relationship of all the colors together rather than any attempt to match each tone separately with its original in the subject. It is therefore best to stand back from the painting at each new stage to check the overall effect.

Materials

Surface
Stretched and primed cotton duck

Size
24in × 30in (60cm × 75cm)

Tools
Nos 3, and 11 flat bristle brushes

Colors

Black	Hooker's green
Burnt sienna	Lemon yellow
Burnt umber	Pthalo crimson
Cadmium red medium	Ultramarine
Cadmium yellow medium	White
Chrome green	

Medium
Water

Outlining · underpainting warm tones

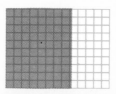

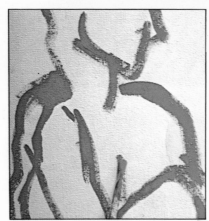

Figure outlines are sketched in with a bold red before blocking in predominant color tones. The outlines are later covered over; however, the red continues to permeate successive layers, warming tones.

Blocking in an underpainting of warm pinks and oranges. This layer is later used for warm highlight areas or covered over with cool tones of green and blue.

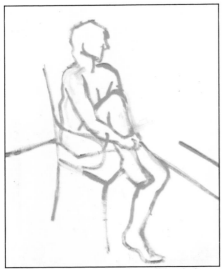

1.Use a No 3 bristle brush, well loaded with cadmium red to draw in the outline of the figure. Correct the shape and work over the alterations in white if necessary.

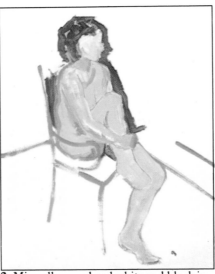

2. Mix yellow, red and white and block in the flesh tones. Lay in a dark green behind the figure to form the basic background.

3. Lay in thin layers of color covering more of the canvas. Continue to work on the figure with pinks and browns and use green for the shadows.

4. Use a No 11 brush to cover the whole background with a thin wash of green. Describe the foliage shapes in yellow and add details to the chair.

5. Block in leaf shapes with green and yellow mixtures, working into the shadows with black and burnt sienna.

6. Work around the figure covering all the remaining white space and elaborating background forms. Lighten the floor color with blue-grey.

7. Draw the chair in more detail with burnt umber, adding highlights in white and dark tones in black.

8. Work over the figure using a light flesh tone and put in shadows in green. Describe the shadow under the chair with a thin layer of black.

9. Rework parts of the figure as needed, refining the shapes and emphasizing tonal contrast. Bring up the white of the cushion with thick paint.

PAINTING CAN BE a matter of moment-by-moment decision: not all studies need be meticulously planned. In this picture some of the forms, and indeed the structure of the composition as a whole, underwent radical changes as the work progressed. The drawing was continuously redrafted with whole figures as well as small details vanishing under a layer of paint and re-emerging at a later stage. The overall structure was completely altered when the flat, distant horizon line was cut short by the tall block of buildings. The artist chose to do this to close off the picture space and force the observer's eye into the cluster of figures in the mid- and foreground areas.

The painting was constructed from a number of photographs, with the artist taking single figures and groups from different sources to create a composite image. Thus the artist felt complete freedom to experiment and develop the structure in any way which interested him.

Making such alterations in a painting is not unusual and the development of a quick-drying paint such as acrylic has given artists a great deal of freedom in this respect.

Paint out the forms with a solid layer of color and draw them again in outline with the point of the brush. As you become more confident you may prefer to rework directly in color over previous shapes.

Materials

Surface
Prepared canvas board

Size
28in × 24in (70cm × 60cm)

Tools
No 8 sable round brush
Nos 4 and 6 round bristle brushes
Palette

Colors
Black	Cadmium yellow
Burnt sienna	Cobalt blue
Cadmium green	Ultramarine blue
Cadmium lemon	Viridian
Cadmium orange	White
Cadmium red medium	Yellow ochre

Mediums
Water
Acrylic matt medium

1. Start to block in figures with dryish paint, drawing the brush lightly across the surface of the canvas board.

2. Scrub over the sky with ultramarine and the beach with warm oranges and yellows. Draw over the colors with fine black lines.

6. Adjust the drawing freely, working over the shapes to try out different compositional arrangements.

7. Concentrate on developing details in one group of figures, gradually improving the modelling of the forms and tones.

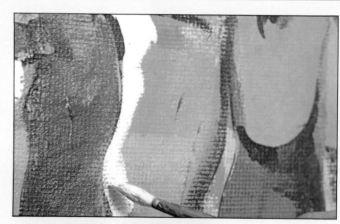

When the underpainting has completely dried, the artist blocks in strong highlight areas with pure white and a small brush.

Working from dark to light, the artist begins to lay in light flesh tones over the dark, warm underpainting.

3. Work into the figures on the right side with orange, brown, and black.

4. Lighten the tone of the sky and at the same time lower the horizon line. Work into the foreground with pale tones and white, adding small details.

5. Continue to develop the figures and main shapes with fine black outlines and blocks of strong, light color.

8. If necessary, make changes in the composition. Here the painting has been strengthened by the addition of a group of buildings.

9. Rework the figures in the foreground building up the contrast of light and dark colors. Block out shapes with a layer of thin, pale orange.

10. Lay in glazes of red over the flesh tones. Develop the shadows with black and grey.

Finished picture · highlights · dark to light

The artist continued to make radical changes in the painting until the very end. This is clearly seen in the figure in the foreground right; the change of position and addition of the yellow jacket add liveliness and interest to the picture.

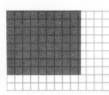

MANY ARTISTS CHOOSE to paint the figure in isolation – without background or props – the better to concentrate on the form, shape, and colour of the model. However, it is important for artists to also consider using the environment around the model to emphasize the figure and create an interesting image. As seen in this painting, not only is the figure itself successfully described, but the area outside the figure is given equal attention as well, which heightens the impact of the picture as a whole.

The painting has successfully captured a strong impression of light and shadow and revolves around a theme of contrasts – the geometric lines and planes of the environment and the cold, bright light coming through the window. This contrasts with the warm, soft figure. The everyday world beyond the window heightens the intimacy of the subject and setting within and creates a visually stimulating idea.

Materials

Surface
Tinted watercolor paper

Size
24in × 26in (62cm × 65cm)

Tools
Nos 2 and 4 sable watercolor brushes
Rags or tissues
Palette

Colors

Black	Chrome green
Burnt sienna	White
Cadmium red	Yellow ochre
Cadmium yellow	

Medium
Water

Finished picture · underpainting · using masking tape

To finish the picture, the artist cleaned up broad areas of color and strengthened the view outside the window. Note as well that the picture was cropped (above), thus strengthening the composition and focus of the image.

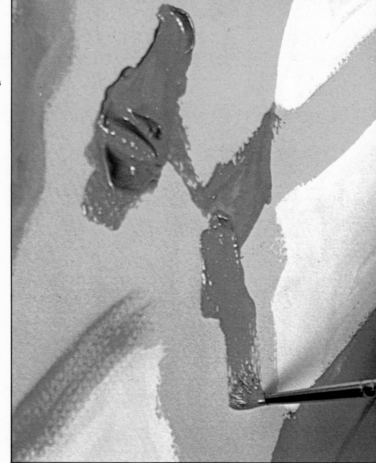

Besides creating sharp, straight edges, masking tape can be used as a mask to describe irregular shapes and patterns. Here the artist paints over two pieces of torn tape to create the rough edge of the window.

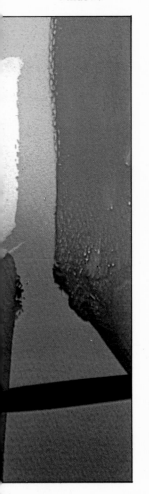

Shadow areas within the figure are blocked in directly with burnt sienna. The color and shape is later modified by overpainting with warmer, lighter flesh tones.

1. In thick, opaque white, block in highlight areas with a No 4 brush. Add black to the white and put in shadow areas.

3. With a deeper grey mixture, put in verticals and horizontals. Mix white and yellow and put in figure highlights.

5. In dark grey, block in the dark shadow area behind the figure. With cadmium red, put in bus outside of the window.

2. Mix chrome green and cadmium yellow pale and block in shape of window. In burnt sienna, block in the shadow area of the figure.

4. Using a No 2 sable brush, work back into the figure with the dark grey tones. Mix cadmium red and white and block in the figure.

6. In loose strokes add touches of detail outside the window.

Watercolor

IN THIS PAINTING, strong patterns of light and shade introduce an abstract element to an otherwise straightforward pose. The tone and color contrasts form an intricate network of shapes which are emphasized to build up the image piece by piece. The figure is basically composed of warm tones of orange, yellow, and brown and are given extra brilliance by the cool, dark blues of surrounding colors. These colors are linked across the image with the warm mauve and intense blue-purple in the shadows of the figure and the background. The strong green of the floor is an unexpected departure from the overall color scheme and provides a lively base for the composition.

The painting technique is fluid and vigorous. Large pools of color are laid down to establish the general shapes, which are then broken down by successive applications of smaller patches of wet color. Use round sable brushes with a relaxed, flowing stroke; a great part of the appeal of the image is that no shape is absolutely precise. To make the most of the colors, dry the painting frequently so that the effect of the overlapping washes is not diffused.

Materials

Surface
Stretched cartridge paper

Size
9.5in × 15in (24cm × 37cm)

Tools
No 5 sable round brush
Colored pencils   2B pencil

Colors

Burnt umber	Scarlet lake
Cadmium yellow	Ultramarine blue
Cobalt blue	*Pencils*
Emerald green	Blue
Orange	Orange
Purple	Purple
Magenta	

Medium
Water

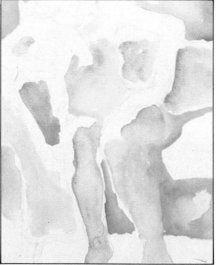

1. Sketch in a rough guideline for the painting with a 2B pencil. Lay in shadows with thin washes of paint using warm colors.

2. Work into the figure with yellow and violet developing the pattern of light and shade. Put in the floor with a wash of emerald green, blues and purples.

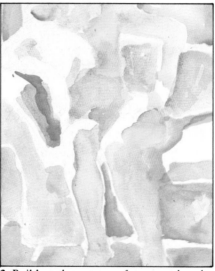

3. Build up the contrast of warm and cool tones in the figure, blocking in small patches of color to describe shadows.

4. Mix the paint with less water to intensify the dark tones. Break down the large shapes to show details such as facial features and the fingers on the hand.

5. Work over the skin tones with small shapes of burnt sienna and burnt umber. Overlap the colors and drop in touches of blue to vary the dark tones.

6. When the paint is dry, work over the forms with colored pencils, modifying the shapes and tones.

Lifting color with tissue · overlaying with colored pencils

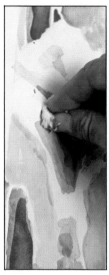

To lighten a color tone, a small piece of tissue can be used to lift the paint. Do not rub into the surface but simply blot with the tissue.

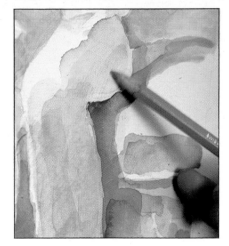

After the painting has dried, colored pencils may be used to create subtle overlays of color. Here the artist strengthen shadow areas in the legs using a blue pencil over a warm color area.

WATERCOLOR IS AN excellent medium for painting a nude, as its delicacy and transparency are particularly suited to the task of building up subtle variations of flesh tones. Color is gradually intensified and broken down into smaller areas with light tones created by the bare white surface of the paper.

To create a balanced composition, the figure has been placed to one side of the paper with the head turned to look across the picture space. The dark, heavy background area adds emphasis to light colors and details within the figure. The model's hat gives a splash of bright color against the subtle flesh tones and cool blue and grey of the surrounding area.

The success of this type of painting depends upon accurate, direct drawing with a good sable brush. Work on each form separately to build up details and make adjustments in the final stages to unify the overall effect. Each shape should be carefully observed and then precisely applied. Keep the paint thin and light as it is difficult to lift off color which has been applied too thickly. It is advisable to dry the painting frequently by either letting the moisture evaporate naturally, fanning the picture, or using a hair dryer so the colors do not mix and become muddy. Brushes should be kept clean and water pots refilled at regular intervals during the work.

Materials

Surface
Stretched watercolor paper

Size
20in × 16in (50cm × 40cm)

Tools
Nos 3 and 6 sable round brushes
No 10 flat ox-ear brush
1in (2.5cm) decorators' brush

Colors

Black	Cobalt blue
Burnt sienna	Light red
Cadmium red	Payne's grey
Cadmium yellow	Scarlet lake

Medium
Water

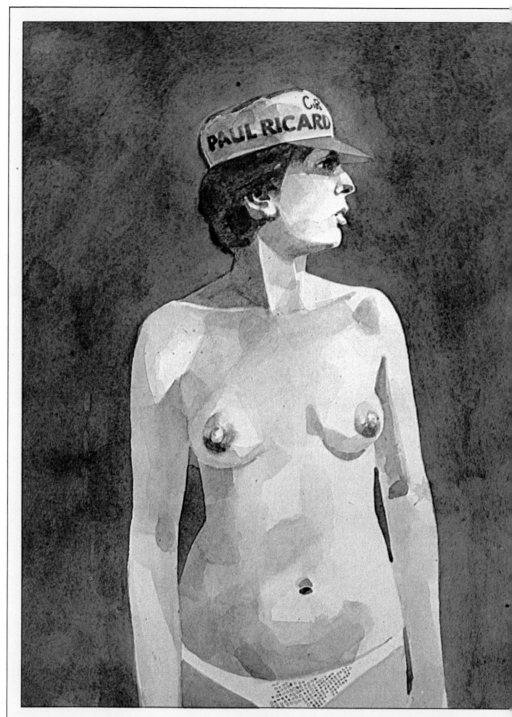

Detailing with pencil

A fine-pointed, dark pencil is here being used to create texture and pattern in the model's pants.

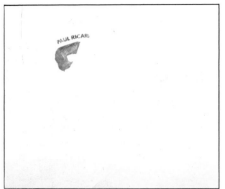

1. Lightly pencil in the outline of the figure and with a No 3 brush paint in the darkest details with black. Lay in a very thin wash of light red with a No 10 brush.

2. Paint in small areas of bright pattern on the cap, keeping the colors clean and distinct. With a No 3 brush and black, brush into the cap to indicate shadows.

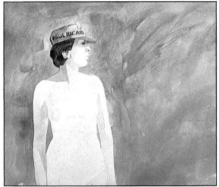

3. Gradually build up skin tones with thin washes of paint, varying the color mixtures and overlaying washes.

4. Use a large No 6 brush to apply a wash of color across the background, with a mixture of cobalt blue and Payne's grey. Follow the outline of the figure carefully.

5. Strengthen the shadows in the figure, preserving highlights and light tones. Lay light washes of scarlet lake.

6. Intensify the background color, adding a little black to the blue and grey mixture.

7. Adjust the tones of the figure against the dark background, bringing up details of the features and adding small shapes of dark color to show strong shadows.

8. Work over the whole image to define the full volume of the head and body, using thin washes of black and red to sharpen detail and enliven color.

THE ATMOSPHERIC MOOD of this picture was achieved through the subtle overlaying of washes of color and a dramatic use of light and shadow.

Within the figure, this method of painting mimics the actual physical makeup of the human body. The 'color' of human flesh is created by the many thousands of small arteries and veins carrying blood and oxygen and layer upon layer of tissue and pigment as well. Flesh tone is a translucent 'color' created by these many layers. All of these elements could be thought of as the 'underpainting' of the human figure by which are created what we call the 'flesh tones'.

It is important to bear in mind that the initial washes of color, no matter how often covered over, will influence the final picture. In this case, the artist used a warm, light tone for the underpainting of the figure knowing that this would keep the figure warm in tone, regardless of the colors put down over this initial layer. The white area falling across the figure creates a dramatic contrast to the general dark and sombre tone of the rest of the picture. The square of white in the background is linked with this white area, joining foreground and background and providing unity.

Materials

Surface
Stretched watercolor paper

Size
21.5in × 14in (53cm × 35cm)

Tools
Nos 4 and 12 sable watercolor brushes
Palette

Colors

Alizarin crimson	Indigo
Burnt umber	Payne's grey
Cadmium lemon	Prussian blue
Cadmium scarlet	Rose madder
Chrome green	Yellow ochre

Medium
Water

1. Sketch in figure in outline. Dampen background area and spread wet mixture of indigo and cadmium yellow. Mix cadmium and yellow and put in figure.

2. When dry, mix wash of water and Payne's grey and put in bed. Strengthen tone of paint by adding more grey to create dark shadow areas.

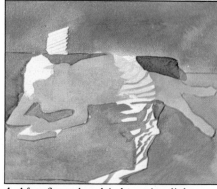

3. Mix Payne's grey and cadmium red light in wet wash and put in floor with a No 12 brush, keeping the tone consistent.

4. After figure has dried, put in a light wash of rose madder with a No 4 brush letting brush and paint describe the subtler flesh tones.

5. Add more red to flesh tone and put in striped shadow area across figure.

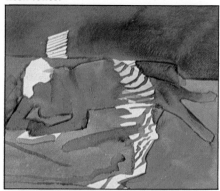

6. Create darker flesh tone by adding a touch of burnt umber. With Payne's grey, describe shadow area in bed and window. Put wash of yellow over figure.

7. Mix a dark shade of chrome green and flood in over the background color with the No 12 brush.

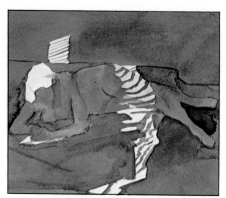

8. With a dark mixture of Payne's grey and water, put in deep shadow tones in bed and under figure's feet.

Using warm wash · wet-in-wet · shadow details

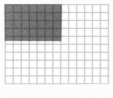

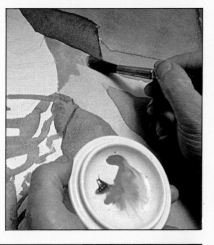

Mixing paint in small dishes which can be held in the hand allows the artist to work quickly. Here the artist is overpainting the initial yellow layer in the figure's legs with a warm red.

Working over the slightly damp underpainting, the artist lays in thin lines of dark paint to describe the shadow over the figure.

One way of working wet-in-wet is to lay down a small area of color (above) and then immediately flood this with a clean brush and water. If too much water is applied, this is easily lifted with a small piece of tissue or cotton. Remember not to rub into the surface, but simply blot up the excess moisture (left).

WORKING QUICKLY WITH only a few colors and brushes, the artist has here created a fascinating picture which fulfills all the requirements of a successful figure study. Using more than one figure is always an interesting exercise. The artist can combine sketches of different poses into one painting, but make sure the lighting is similar to avoid confusion.

Using a grey underpainting to set the mood and tone of the picture, the artist worked from dark to light with wet paint; each layer grew more opaque with the addition of designer's white gouache into the flesh tones. In some areas the wet paint was allowed to bleed and blend into a previous wet area; in other areas a dryish, opaque mixture was put over a dry layer.

Note in particular how the artist has used just a few warm and cool tones to create a variety of shades within the figure. The subtle colours are contrasted with the sharp, intense black areas of the hair and the shadow areas outside of the figures.

Compositionally, the painting presents a balanced and symmetrical image by placing the figures in such a way that the eye is led downward and into the centre of the picture plane.

Materials

Surface
Stretched watercolor paper

Size
20in × 16in (50cm × 40cm)

Tools
Small sponge
Nos 6, 12 sable round watercolor brushes

Colors
Alizarin crimson	Payne's grey
Cadmium red light	White (gouache)
Chrome green	Yellow ochre

Medium
Water

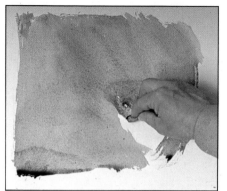

1. Mix a large amount of Payne's grey and water in a mixing dish and with a small sponge work over the painting surface.

2. With a No 12 brush, work back into the underpainting with a darker tone of grey, blocking in dark areas around the figures.

3. While still wet, use a No 12 brush and chrome green and block in the shadow areas of the first figure. Mix white, ochre and red for highlights.

4. Work down the figure with opaque white and yellow ochre mixture.

5. Block in the hair with pure Payne's grey and the highlights with pure white using a No 6 brush.

6. With the same flesh tones, put in the figure on the right with lighter colors made by adding white.

7. Put in dark details of hair and shadow areas, allowing the paint to bleed into previous area.

8. Mix Payne's grey and water and block in shadow areas around the figures.

Laying in highlights

Working into the
slightly damp
underpainting, the
artist develops
strong highlight
areas.

Tempera

WHILE TEMPERA PAINTING has never quite regained the widespread popularity it enjoyed with the artists of medieval times, it is still used by many contemporary painters as a fascinating and challenging alternative to other painting media.

When used as an underpainting for an oil painting, tempera will give a glowing, translucent effect. Once the oil paint layer has dried thoroughly, the artist can return to working with tempera if he chooses.

If dry pigments are used, tempera colors will not necessarily dry as they look when applied to the surface; they may dry lighter or darker depending on the type of pigment used. For this reason it is a good idea to test colors on a separate piece of similar surface before beginning to work.

An important point to note is that tempera cannot be easily corrected or overpainted during the painting process. Thus, this process requires planning and forethought. Small areas should be worked on one at a time, allowing each layer to dry thoroughly before beginning the next.

Materials

Surface
Primed hardboard sized with muslin

Size
24in × 20in (60cm × 50cm)

Tools
No 2 sable brush
Small jar
Piece of flannel
Plate

Colors (dry pigments)
Black   Viridian
Cobalt blue   White
Light red   Yellow ochre
Terre verte

Mediums
Egg yolk
Water

1. Transfer the preliminary sketch on to a board by placing the sketch drawing side down and rubbing over the back with a soft dark pencil.

2. Mix light red with some egg yolk, and with a No 2 brush, put in red areas using very light, fluid strokes.

3. Using terre verte and viridian in varying tones of green, put in figure shadows using the same light touch.

4. Work over the whole picture with these same tones. Mix only the amount needed and change brushes depending on the area to be covered.

5. Darken tones of green by adding a small amount of blue pigment and work over previous areas, intensifying shadows.

6. Continue to strengthen and blend green background tones. Work into the figures with ochre, beginning to put in the various highlight areas.

7. Develop small areas of detail, such as the tree on the left, with a dark blue-green tone. Use only the tip of the brush to touch in colors.

8. Using pure cobalt blue, strengthen outlines and shadows in this same detail area.

Underpainting with terre verte · using white

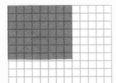

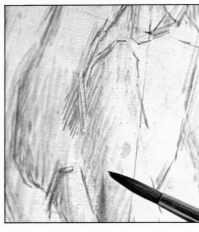

Here the artist is putting in a cool underpainting in terre verte. Note the directional strokes and the light touch required.

At a more advanced stage, white mixed with yolk can be used to tone down previous color areas. White can also be used to correct and rework, but the color laid over this will lose some of its translucence in the process.

Pastel

PASTEL drawing requires a combination of drawing and painting skills. It can be treated either as a linear medium for outlines and loosely hatched textures, or the color may be laid in broad, grainy patches and blended with the fingers or a rag. Pastel color is soft and powdery and, although it is held together by the tooth of the paper, the surface is always unstable. The drawing should be sprayed with fixative frequently to hold the image while further layers are applied.

The rich textures are built up in a series of overlaid marks, carefully manipulated to describe the forms in terms of their component shapes and color relationships. In this drawing, the pastel strokes have a vertical emphasis, but sometimes marks follow the direction of the forms in order to emphasize a particular curve or angle. It is easier to control the overall image if the strokes follow one direction. In the initial stages of the drawing use medium soft pastels, graduating to the soft type to develop texture as the drawing progresses.

Materials

Surface
Tinted rag paper

Size
23in × 30in (57cm × 75cm)

Tools
Fixative

Colors

Black	Light yellow
Cobalt blue	Olive green
Dark brown	Red
Flesh	Venetian red
Grey	Ultramarine blue

1. Mark the position of the head and limbs with a pink pastel tint and roughly block in the structure of the figure with pink, light yellow, brown and grey.

2. Work lightly over the whole figure, weaving colors together so basic shapes and tones begin to emerge. Use grey and blue to suggest dark tones.

4. Develop cool tones in the drapery with light blue and white and darken the background color with broad vertical strokes of olive green and ultramarine.

5. Work over the composition with tones of grey to strengthen shadows. Draw into the figure with light yellow and dark red to build up the solidity of the form.

7. Intensify the blues in the background, laying in brown and green to vary the color. Develop the colors over the whole drawing, altering if necessary.

8. Emphasize highlights with yellow and white and lighten the background colour with cobalt blue and white. Add touches of warm pink tones into the drapery.

3. Spray the work lightly with fixative. Start to build up a contrast of cool and warm tones using blue and green in the shadow areas.

6. Overlay the colors so that the pastel strokes remain visible but the image works as a whole form. Work over the figure to heighten the tonal contrasts.

9. Round out the forms of the figure using a dark flesh pink, contrasted with cool green in the shadows. Use pinks and browns to warm the drawing.

Finished picture · blocking in · using pure color

As seen in the finished picture, it is the combination of forceful, vertical strokes used to define a largely horizontal subject which creates a harmonious, stable image.

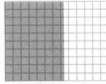

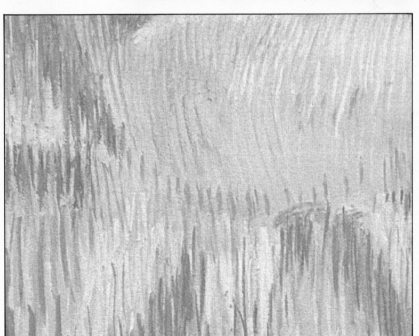

Thin lines of pure color are laid down in directional strokes next to and on top of one another.

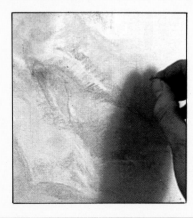

In the first few stages of drawing, the artist describes large areas of color using the side of the chalk.

IN COMMON with watercolor, pastels allow the artist to create layers of transparent colour. These can be used either to subtly imply warm or cool tones or to indicate shadow or highlight areas.

The picture here relies basically on the use of warm and cool tones to create the flesh tones and give the picture unity. The artist worked by developing highlights and shadows, constantly adjusting and readjusting these to correct the balance of warm and cool colors.

Note that pastel cannot be easily erased. If you use a light hand throughout the drawing process, however, you will avoid building up a heavy and unworkable surface.

Compositionally, the drawing was planned to focus attention on the head of the model rather tham the complete torso. By leaving the figure relatively untouched except for a few sparse outlines, and working well into the head and background areas, the artist ensured that the viewer's attention would be focused on the head – the most important area of the picture.

Materials

Surface
Cartridge paper

Size
18.5in × 26in (47cm × 65cm)

Tools
Large soft brush
2B pencil
Putty eraser
Fixative

Colors
Light grey
Dark grey
Black
White

1. Reinforce pencil outlines with pastel. Use a deep tone for the hair and shadow areas of the face.

2. Continue to sketch in the figure in loose outline and block in the background and figure using the same tone.

3. Lighten the background area and carry this tone into the face. With a soft brush blend the background and face.

4. Heighten shadow areas in the face with a deeper tone and work into highlights with a lighter tone.

5. Describe background in more detail and carry this tone into the hair area. Blend the face with a large, soft brush.

6. Using pure white, cover the face area with directional strokes and blend with the brush.

Using pure white · blending with brush

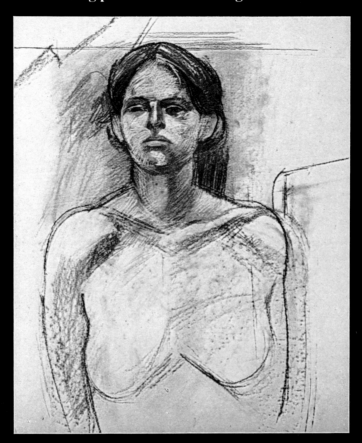

Besides using a rag or fingers to blend, a large, soft sable brush is a useful tool. The artist is here blending strong highlight tones into the darker underlayer.

Using pure white, the artist lays in strong strokes which will be blended and modified by other colors. Note the use of directional strokes to model the face.

Pencil

MUCH LIKE CRAYONS, colored pencils are often overlooked as an exciting drawing medium. As seen in this drawing, they are capable of producing brilliant colors and dramatic tones. The picture is interesting not only for the techniques used in describing the form, but for the unusual and striking composition as well.

In terms of technique, the artist used a combination of heavy, dense shadow areas and lighter, translucent highlights. These play off one another to both heighten and modify the overall effect of the picture. Note that the drawing process is very similar to the traditional oil painting process; thin layers of pure color are laid over one another to build up a shimmering, translucent surface. While it appears that many individual tones and colors have been used, the artist has in fact used only a few warm and cool colors. The flesh tone is used all over the figure and altered for highlight and shadow areas by either overlaying warm red tones for highlights or cool blues for shadows.

Compositionally, the artist has exploited the white of the paper, using it to become part of the drawing as demonstrated in the playing cards and sunglasses. This is extremely effective in creating unity between the image and its environment, as well as strengthening the intensity of colored areas.

Materials

Surface
Cartridge paper

Size
14in14in (35cm × 35cm)

Tools
Putty eraser

Colors

Black	Pale blue
Blue-violet	Purple
Green	Red
Orange	Yellow

1. Sketch in the figure very lightly with a 2B pencil. With heavy strokes, put in the hair in black and light blue outside of the head. Mix black and red in the glasses.

2. Overlay thin layers of purple and blue in the shoulder areas.

3. Work over the shoulder with a thin layer of orange. Move down the arm and breast, again leaving the paper bare to describe white areas. Carry blue shadow down.

4. With cool blue or purple and overlaying warm flesh tones, put in the right shoulder. Very loosely describe the blue shadow at the right of the head.

5. Varying warm tones of orange, red, and yellow, lightly work down the figure. Continue to use cool blue or purple for shadow areas.

6. Work down over the stomach area with the same warm and cool tones. Keep shadow areas dense and clearly defined.

Finished picture · using white of paper

Colored pencil should not be overlooked as a forceful tool, capable of producing effects equal to any painting medium. The clean, pure color areas contrast well with any tinted or pure white drawing surface.

This detail clearly shows the use of the white paper, rather than color, to create shapes.

FIGURE DRAWING IN pencil is one of the most useful skills for artists to acquire and is usually included in the first projects given in art schools.

Interesting variations can be obtained by placing the figure in strong light and shadow. If the effect of the light is to be the main interest of the drawing, the picture must be treated as a tonal study by taking advantage of the patterns of light and shade across the forms.

Large areas of pencil shading can become either boring or messy, so the tones must be developed gradually and the textures varied to define separate forms. The dense grey background area in this drawing is built up with layers of fine, criss-crossed marks, loosely woven together to create an overall tone. The shading on the figure is more solid and close-knit, and the dark tones are contrasted with the bare white paper representing the fall of the light.

Materials

Surface
Thick cartridge paper

Size
24in × 16in (60cm × 40cm)

Tools
HB and 2B pencils
Putty eraser
Fixative

1. To establish the scale, start by making a brief outline sketch of the figure. Work into the shape of the head, laying in the darkest tones.

2. Strengthen the outline, working down from the head, and block in dark stripes of shadow cutting across the body. Lay a mid-toned grey behind the head.

Describing tone

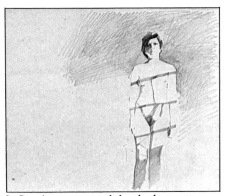  

3. Continue to extend the shadow pattern on the figure with dark shading. Develop the background tone, keeping the marks light and loose.

4. Draw into the background behind the figure, lightly outlining shapes with tonal shading.

5. Complete the area of background tone and work back into the shapes of the figure and shadows, building up details in the forms and patterns.

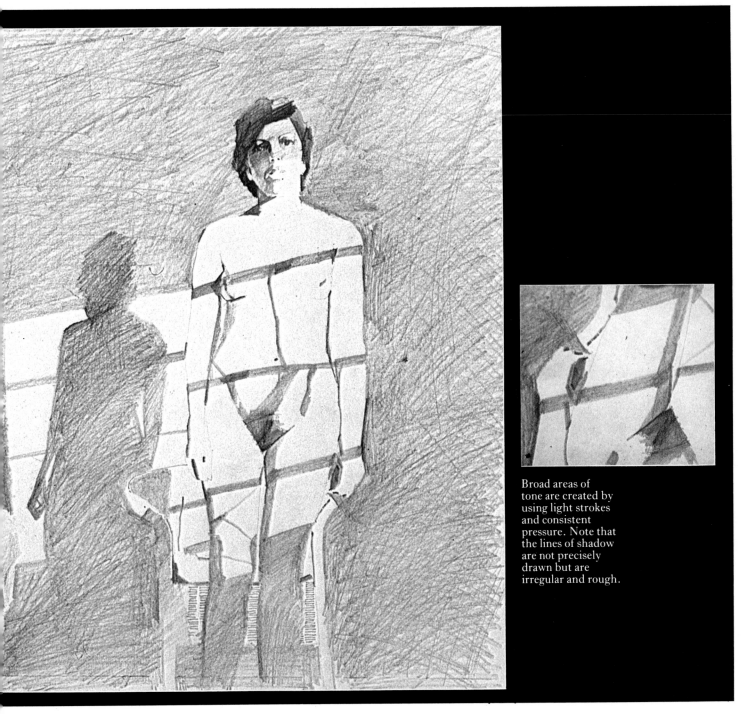

Broad areas of tone are created by using light strokes and consistent pressure. Note that the lines of shadow are not precisely drawn but are irregular and rough.

THE GENERAL impression of this drawing is similar to an old photograph or print due largely to the color of the paper and the soft pencil tones. The picture shows how pencil can be used with a light, subtle touch to create a peaceful, stable atmosphere.

The effect is also similar to the drawings of the French artist Seurat who, by using rough paper and a soft, dark crayon, was able to create tonal areas duplicating the pointillist technique. A rough surface will lessen the linear effect of the pencil and blend tones more evenly than smooth paper.

The artist here depended upon the use of tone to create an illusion of space and depth and, as seen in the head, this can heighten the overall emphasis of the figure within the picture plane. Although most of the page is blank with no indication of the environment, putting the dark shadow area outside the face gives an impression of depth and space.

Materials

Surface
Pumpkin colored pastel paper

Size
16in × 20in (40cm × 50cm)

Tools
2B and 4B pencils
Putty eraser
Tissues
Fixative

1. Lightly sketch in the outlines of the figure with a 2B pencil.

2. Begin very lightly to put in the shadow areas with loose, directional strokes. Add dark details around the neck.

3. Work back into the hair with more pressure, building up darks. Strengthen face and chair outlines.

4. Begin to work outside of the face with very light strokes. Carry this over to the flower shape.

5. Strengthen the shadow areas within the figure. With a 2B pencil, work down the figure, roughing in general outlines and shadow areas.

6. With a 4B pencil, strengthen details of face and flower. With same, darken shadow areas in the dress.

Creating tones with putty eraser

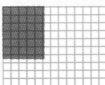

The artist works into the facial details using a combination of grey tones and the clean paper surface to describe shadow and highlight areas.

Creating tones with putty eraser

CHARCOAL IS a most rewarding artistic medium. It gives a characteristic rich, soft black color and a wide variety of textures and tones. However, it is powdery and impermanent, while the drawing may soon become messy and uncontrolled if over elaborated.

Observe the subject carefully as you draw, analysing the shapes and tones, and make your marks decisive and vigorous. Do not attempt to be too precise; a stick of charcoal cannot be as carefully manipulated as the fine point of a pencil, for instance. The best subject is a strong image full of dense tone and calligraphic line. Use a putty eraser both to take out errors and to draw highlights into the loose, black surface. Fix the drawing whenever a stage of the work is successfully completed so that the surface does not become dull and smudgy.

A charcoal drawing on tinted paper can prove particularly effective, especially if white gouache is applied to strengthen the highlights and round out the forms. Use the paint sparingly and keep it free of charcoal dust or it will look dull and grey, deadening the tonal contrasts and producing an opposite effect to the one intended.

Materials

Surface
Tinted drawing paper

Size
16in × 23in (40cm × 57cm)

Tools
No 6 sable round brush
Medium charcoal
Putty eraser
White designers' gouache

Medium
Water

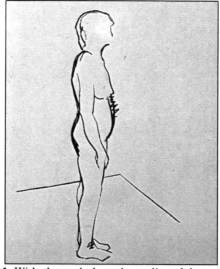

1. With charcoal, draw the outline of the figure with bold, black lines. If necessary, make small corrections or revisions as you work.

2. Start to develop the tonal structure by spreading the charcoal lightly with your fingers and erasing to make grey tones.

3. Lay in broad areas of grey with the side of the charcoal, using the pointed end to draw into the background shapes with loose, calligraphic marks.

4. Block in small areas of solid black around the figure and strengthen the definition of the shapes and patterns with strong lines.

5. Work over the figure adjusting details and strengthening lines. Use the eraser to lighten greys and bring up white highlights.

6. Apply thin patches of white gouache with a No 6 sable brush to add definition to the highlight areas. Let the paint dry before making finishing touches.

52

Highlighting with gouache

With a small brush and white designer's gouache, strong highlights are developed in the figure. The gouache is allowed to blend with the charcoal to create subtle grey tones.

THE OVERALL EFFECT of a drawing executed in pure graphite powder is a subtle, impressionistic one, as if the artist had taken a fleeting glance and quickly described the basic tones and shapes of the subject. Graphite is best used for describing tones, not for creating a highly rendered, detailed drawing. When applied with the fingers, the artist can render the figure in contours and directional strokes which both follow and shape the form.

It is this particular aspect – working in tones rather than line – which gives the medium its unique softness and subtlety. However, pure graphite powder has a slippery quality and, because it is so easily applied to the surface, the artist must avoid losing control of the drawing. If mistakes are made however, they can be easily rubbed out with a rag and turpentine.

When used with turpentine, a range of tones can be created from very pale greys to bold and intense blacks. Coupled with the use of a clean pencil line, the tones of the graphite will lend a soft, atmospheric mood, regardless of subject matter.

Materials

Surface
Heavy weight cartridge paper

Size
14in × 18in (35cm × 45cm)

Tools
4B pencil
Putty eraser
Q-tips
Small rags or tissues

Colors
Raw graphite powder
Cerulean blue pastel

Medium
Turpentine

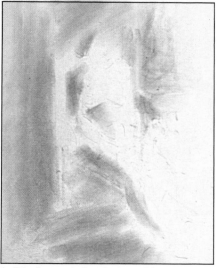

1. Dip fingers in bowl of graphite powder and block in general shadow areas. Rubbing harder will create darker tones.

2. With a 4B pencil, rough in figure outlines and further develop shadows within the figure.

3. Dip a small rag or Q-tip in turpentine and rub on to the surface. Wipe out mistakes or false highlights with a clean rag and turpentine.

4. Dip a clean Q-tip in graphite and work around the figure, darkening the background.

5. Darken the background to bring out light areas. Reinforce figure outlines in pencil. Work around the figure with a rag dipped in turpentine.

Drawing with fingers · blending with turpentine

The fingers are first dipped into the pure graphite powder and then applied directly on to the drawing surface. The pressure and amount of powder will determine the density of tone.

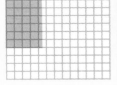

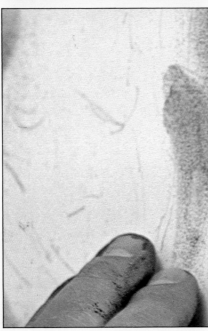

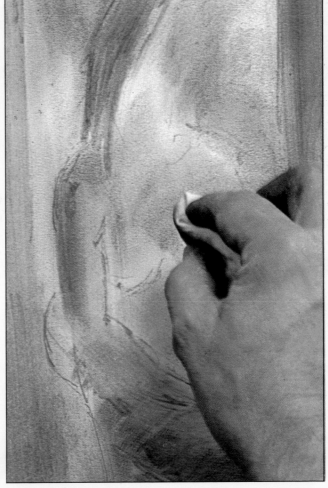

With a small tissue dipped in turpentine, the graphite can be blended and worked to create a variety of tones.

Pen and ink

WHILE PEN AND ink may at first prove uncomfortable and awkward to work with, the artist will soon develop a natural feel for the movement of the pen, the flow of the ink, and which gestures produce which marks. The pen and ink draftsman creates a draw-drawing from the use of the white of the paper, the black of the ink, and the many tones in between these two. These tones are usually created by the use of individual lines of ink which, when laid over one another in various directions, create a mesh-like effect, giving an impression of shadow and depth. Unlike other drawing and painting media, the pen and ink artist is limited to the use of line for de-veloping tone, but, as demonstrated in this drawing, creating a highly model-led, accurate drawing presents no problem despite this limitation.

In this drawing, the artist, with a minimum of detail, has accurately rendered the figure. The simple use of outline and shaded, crosshatched areas alone gives the figure shape, dimension and weight. The tone cre-ated by pen and ink can be very subtly varied and need not have a harsh black and white effect, if carefully graduated and controlled. If you look carefully at the area of the hand resting on the knee, you will see that only loose, rough strokes have been used to de-scribe the shadow areas.

Materials

Surface
Smooth cartridge paper

Size
9in × 12in (22cm × 30cm)

Tools
Dip pen
Fine nib
2B pencil

Colors
Black waterproof ink

1. Sketch in the figure very roughly with a 2B pencil. Put in general outlines in ink and begin to describe shadow areas.

2. Continue the outline of the figure and return to put in shadow areas. Use a hatching stroke to define muscles.

3. Continue outline of the arm. Moving outside of the figure, very loosely put in broad strokes, working in one direction.

4. Continue down to hands and legs of figure, putting in outlines and then working into shadow areas with light strokes.

5. Carry background tone down behind the chair using same directional strokes. Leave white of paper bare to define chair shape.

6. Changing the direction of the line, put in general shadow over the leg. Crosshatch over the background shadow to create a denser tone.

Defining shadow areas

Broad areas of
light hatching are
defined by using a
dark outline to
enclose the strokes.

WHILE A large variety of commercial pens and nibs are available, it is interesting to experiment with hand-cut pens made from quills or hollow sticks. A thick reed pen is used here to give a bold, fluid line to create a spontaneous image.

Drawing with line will give the basic outlines of the forms; the image is then given volume by loose washes of thin, wet color. A rich surface texture can be built up with this technique so, although only two colors have been used in this picture, a considerable variety of tonal density is achieved.

The intention is not to depict the subject in meticulous detail, but to record a lively impression of the mood and pose which exploits the freedom and diversity of the medium. If the pen is used on dry paper, or over a dry wash it makes a strong, sharp line. When line is applied into wet layers they will spread and feather. Be careful when drawing into a wet area not to tear the damp paper with the point of the pen. Vary the shapes and tones of the washes to provide a contrast between hard-edged shapes and subtly blended tones so that the full versatility of the medium contributes to the overall effect.

Materials

Surface
Stretched cartridge paper

Size
18in × 22in (45cm × 55cm)

Tools
Hollow piece of reed or willow
Knife or scalpel
No 8 round sable brush

Colors
Brown ink
Black waterproof India ink

Medium
Water

1. Dip the pen in black ink diluted with water and draw the profile of the head. Using a small sable brush, apply thin washes of brown ink.

2. Continue to build up the washes, preserving areas of white. Use the pen to define the linear shapes in the foreground and background.

Making the reed pen · the pen line

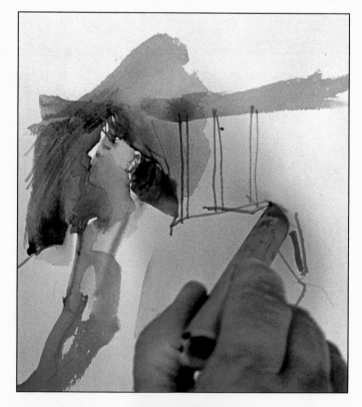

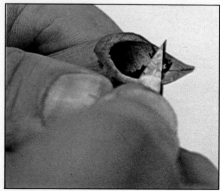

A reed pen can be made from any type of hollow wood. Once roughly shaped, the point is refined with a small knife. The line created by a reed pen is irregular yet soft and produces an effect very suitable for figure work.

3. Lay in broad washes of diluted brown and black inks, working across the entire picture.

4. Draw the figure in more detail using bold, fluid lines. Enrich the shadows with additional washes of brown and black ink.

5. Strengthen linear detail and dark tones with the pen and brush in black.

A rapidograph was used for this drawing rather than the traditional pen, nib, and ink as it gives a more consistent line. Thus the artist could develop fine areas of crosshatching without fear of dripping. By leaving the white paper untouched for highlight areas and using hatching and crosshatching to describe shadow areas, the artist has created an interesting drawing.

The rapidograph is a sensitive and temperamental tool. The artist must have a light touch and hold the pen nearly upright to keep the ink flowing. The pen should be shaken frequently in this position to make sure the nib does not clog. The paper used with a rapidograph should have a very smooth surface, otherwise the fine hairs of the paper will rip and clog the nib.

Until familiar with the rapidograph, it is worthwhile to experiment with the various textural effects available. Note that in this drawing the artist has used small areas of crosshatching to build up the shadow area, changing the direction of the line to avoid building it up too densely. A huge variety of textures can be created by simply varying the direction and thickness of the line.

Materials

Surface
Cartridge paper

Size
12in × 23in (30cm × 57.5cm)

Tools
Rapidograph
02 nib

Colors
Black rapidograph ink

1. Carry the outline down the figure with the same consistent pressure.

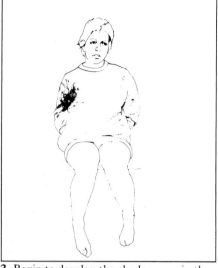

2. Begin to develop the shadow area in the elbow by lightly hatching and crosshatching in small areas, working the line in different directions.

3. Work over the figure and hair developing shadow areas. Watch the balance of light and dark carefully and move back to judge tones.

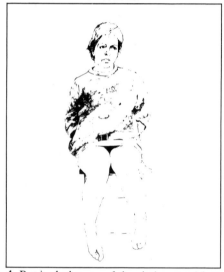

4. Put in dark areas of the chair seat with dense crosshatching.

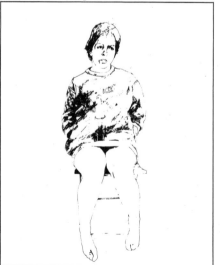

5. Work into the face, and with a very light stroke, put in the shadow areas.

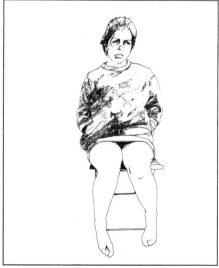

6. Continue to work on the shirt and head, heightening dark areas by overlaying strokes in different directions.

Crosshatching to create tone

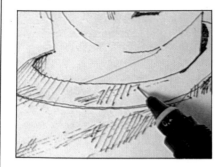

Whether a
rapidograph or
traditional dip type,
the pen relies on the
use of line to create
tone and texture.
Here the use of fine
lines of hatching and
crosshatching are
being used to create
subtle tones and
shadow areas.

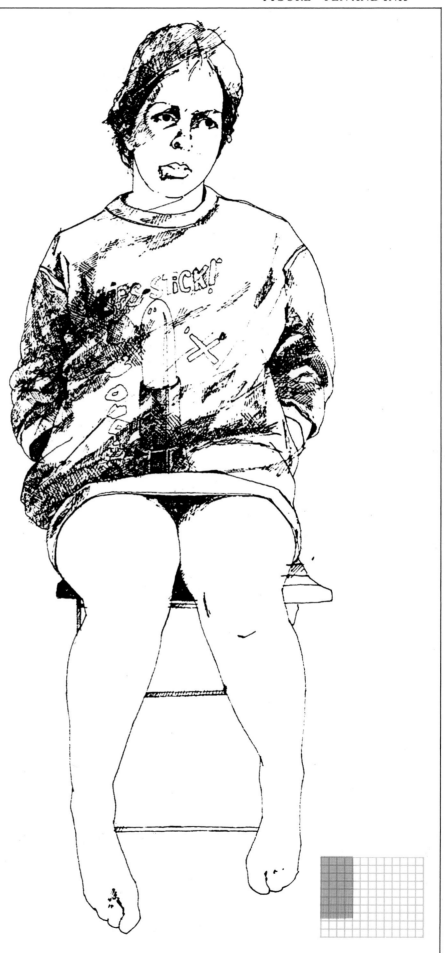